0 00 30 0313744 9

Linking art to the world around us

# Arty Facts

# Planet Earth
## & Art Activities

Crabtree Publishing Company
www.crabtreebooks.com

# Crabtree Publishing Company

PMB 16A, 350 Fifth Avenue, Suite 3308
New York, NY
10118

612 Welland Avenue
St. Catharines, Ontario
L2M 5V6

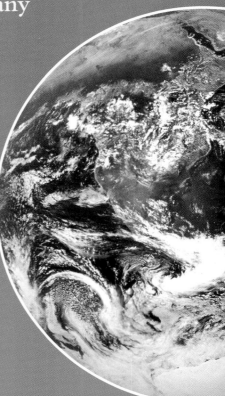

Coordinating Editor: Ellen Rodger
Project Editors: P.A. Finlay, Carrie Gleason
Production Coordinator: Rosie Gowsell
Proofreading, Indexing: Wendy Scavuzzo

Project Development and Concept Marshall Direct:
Editorial Project Director: Karen Foster
Editors: Claire Sippi, Hazel Songhurst, Samantha Sweeney
Researchers: Gerry Bailey, Alec Edgington
Design Director: Tracy Carrington
Designers: Claire Penny, Paul Montague,
James Thompson, Mark Dempsey,
Production: Victoria Grimsell, Christina Brown
Photo Research: Andrea Sadler
Illustrator: Jan Smith
Model Artists: Sophie Dean, Sue Partington, Abigail Dean

Prepress, printing and binding by Worzalla Publishing Company

Cooper, John
   Planet earth and art activities
(Arty facts)
Includes index.
ISBN 0-7787-1111-0 (bound).--ISBN 0-7787-1139-0 (pbk.)
   1. Handicraft--Juvenile literature.  2. Geology in art--Juvenile
literature.  3. Geology--Juvenile literature.  I. Title.  II. Series: Arty facts

QE29.C66 2002              j745.5              C2002-900377-6

Created by
Marshall Direct Learning

FRONT COVER IMAGES: NASA/ SCIENCE PHOTO LIBRARY; MARTIN BARRAUD/ TONY STONE IMAGES: NASA; KRAFFT/ HOA-QUI/ SCIENCE PHOTO LIBRARY

Linking art to the world around us

# Arty Facts

# Planet Earth
## & Art Activities

# Contents

| | | | | |
|---|---|---|---|---|
| Earthgrid | 4 | Rock sculptures | 28 |
| Core and crust | 6 | Stone icicles | 30 |
| Time zones | 8 | Iron and bronze | 32 |
| Drifting lands | 10 | Gemstones | 34 |
| Wrinkles and ridges | 12 | Marvelous metals | 36 |
| Earthquake! | 14 | Silver and gold | 38 |
| Firecones | 16 | Mottled marble | 40 |
| Steam fountains | 18 | Clay soldiers | 42 |
| Striped layers | 20 | Poles apart | 44 |
| Fossil features | 22 | Glossary | 46 |
| Oil, coal, and gas | 24 | Index | 47 |
| Shifting sands | 26 | Materials guide | 48 |

**WRITTEN BY John A. Cooper**

# Earthgrid

The first maps of the world looked very different from the maps we use today. This is because many parts of the world had not yet been discovered. The maps were drawn from imagination instead of fact. The Mappa Mundi, pictured below, is one of the oldest surviving maps. It was drawn around 1290 A.D. and shows strange-looking people with large ears living in faraway lands. Today, we have explored all of Earth and have made more accurate maps!

## Looking down

Maps make the round Earth look flat. They are drawn as if you were high in the air, looking straight down at the land. Mapmakers today draw maps using photographs taken from a plane or satellite. A map can show the whole world, or a small part of the Earth in detail.

## Imaginary lines

On a map of the world, lines running across and downward divide the Earth into sections. **Lines of latitude** run across the map from east to west. **Lines of longitude** run down the map, from the North Pole to the South Pole. The **Equator** is a line of latitude that is exactly halfway between the **North Pole** and the **South Pole**. The Arctic Circle and the Antarctic Circle are lines of latitude close to the North and South Poles.

## Colors and symbols

Colors and **symbols** on maps show us information. The symbols show features, such as a forest or a river. Water and the height of the land are usually shown in different colors. The colors and symbols are explained in a box called the key. Some maps have a scale bar to show distances. For example, one inch (2.5 cm) on the map may be equal to 100 feet (30 m) on the land. Many maps also have an arrow pointing north, to show you the direction.

This map was drawn hundreds of years ago. It was based on what explorers knew about the world at that time.

# Earth

## WHAT YOU NEED

- tissue paper
- glitter pen
- glue
- glitter
- colored poster board
- paper
- scissors
- gold paper

**1** Cut colored tissue paper into different sized strips.

**2** Glue the strips onto the paper. Make geometric shapes by overlapping and placing them at different angles.

**3** Add lines with the glitter pen, or glue on strips of gold paper.

You can design and make different patterns with straight lines

**4** Spread glue in one white space. Sprinkle with glitter, or stick on a piece of gold paper.

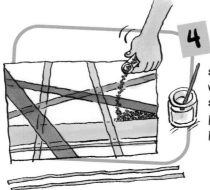

**5** Mount your grid picture on colored poster board.

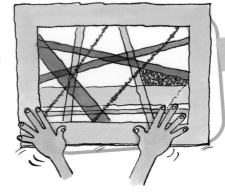

# Core and crust

The Earth is made up of four different layers. The outside layer is like a hard rocky shell. This is called the **crust.** The land and oceans form the top of the crust. Scientists know a lot about this outer layer of the Earth because they have been able to explore it. They do not know as much about the three layers inside the Earth: the **mantle**, the outer core, and the inner core. This is because it would be impossible to explore them deep inside the Earth.

## Guesswork

The crust is up to 25 miles (40 km) thick under mountains and about six miles (10 km) thick under the oceans. Scientists have been able to determine what the inside of the Earth is like from clues found on the crust. Rocks that used to be buried deep have, after billions of years, risen to the surface. Scientists also drilled a borehole into the crust, but it only reached five miles (8 km) deep.

## Hot rock

The mantle has two layers. The upper part is about 404 miles (646 km) thick and made of soft rock. The lower part is 1,364 miles (2,200 km) of packed hot rock. The core begins about 1,802 miles (2,883 km) down. The outer core is hot liquid metal, like thick syrup. The inner core is a hot metal ball about 1,597 miles (2,555 km) thick. It is hard to imagine what it is like inside the Earth. Only 124 miles (200 km) down, the temperature is 2,732°F (1500°C).

# Earth

## WHAT YOU NEED

petroleum jelly

newspaper

paste

double-sided tape

paints and brush

scissors

poster board

black pen

pencil

blow-up beach ball

# Picture globe

**1** Blow up the beach ball and rub petroleum jelly all over it.

**2** Paste several layers of newspaper strips onto the ball. Leave it to dry.

**3** Look at a world map and draw rough outlines of the continents on the globe. Paint the land and oceans.

**4** On the poster board, draw various landmarks, such as buildings, flags, and animals. Paint or color them and cut out with tabs so they can stand up.

**5** Stick them on the globe with double-sided tape.

Where do you live? Make a model of yourself to stick in place on the globe.

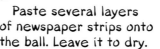
Make a model of your world with added fascinating features

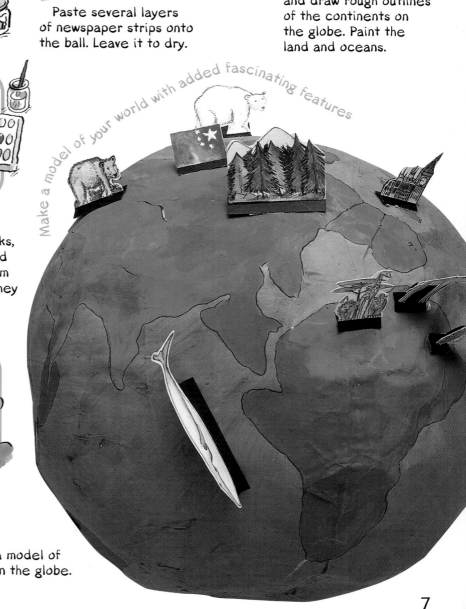

7

# Time zones

A day lasts for 24 hours, but how do you tell if a day has passed if you do not have a clock to measure the time? You can tell by the amount of light or darkness, or the position of the Sun or Moon, in the sky. A year lasts for about 365 days. How do you tell the time of year if you do not have a calendar to count the days? You can tell by the number of daylight hours, since these vary at different times of year.

## Spinning ball

As the Earth travels around the Sun, it spins around an imaginary point that runs through its middle. This imaginary point is called the **axis**. At one end is the North Pole and at the other end is the South Pole. It takes 24 hours for the Earth to complete one spin. The spinning causes day and night. The parts of Earth that face the Sun have daytime, while the parts that face away have night. When it is midday in one part of the world, it is midnight on the opposite side. The spinning movement makes the Sun and Moon appear to travel from east to west across the sky.

## Changing seasons

The length of daylight in a place changes throughout the year, because the slant of the Earth's axis makes one side of the Earth tilt toward the Sun. These different periods of daylight are called seasons. Close to the Equator, the days hardly change at all throughout the year, so there are no seasons. Farther away, most of northern Europe and North America have four seasons. In areas closer to the poles, there are only two seasons. When the North Pole tilts toward the Sun, these areas have constant daylight for about six months. When the North Pole is tilted away from the Sun, there is constant darkness for about six months.

# Earth

## WHAT YOU NEED

poster board

ruler

pencil

paints and brush

glitter

paper fastener

scissors

**1** Cut two circles out of poster board.

**2** Divide one circle into equal sections. In each section, draw or paint a daily activity, such as sleep, mealtime, school, and playtime.

Turn the wheel to reveal your action-packed day and night!

Your disk would look great stuck on the wall, or hung up by a strip of gold or silver thread.

Add sparkle with glitter

**3** Decorate half of the second circle with a sun and half with a moon.

Draw and cut out two cone-shaped sections from the second circle.

**4**

**5** Place the second circle on top, and join them together by pushing a paper fastener through the center.

9

# Drifting lands

The landmass Pangaea starts to break up.

It spreads to form seven separate landmasses.

Three stages of drifting show the final pattern of continents we know today.

Did you know that the Earth's big landmasses, the **continents,** are constantly moving? Each year they move slowly farther apart. Over 130 million years ago, the east coast of South America and the west coast of Africa used to fit together. The mountains in South America were once joined to mountains in South Africa. We know this because the rocks and fossils on both continents are very similar.

## One world

Scientists believe that about 200 million years ago, all the continents were joined in one gigantic continent, which they call **Pangaea**. Over millions of years, this large landmass started to break up, first into two big continents, and finally into seven smaller continents. As the continents split apart, they drifted into the positions they are in today – and they are still moving!

## Earth's plates

The Earth's top layer, the crust, is made up of several enormous, separate pieces called **plates**, which fit together like a giant jigsaw puzzle. The continents and oceans sit on top of these plates. Underneath the plates is a layer of extremely hot liquid rock, called the mantle. The plates float very slowly on the mantle, carrying the seven continents and the oceans in different directions.

## Mountains, earthquakes and volcanoes

When two plates bump into each other, mountains can form as one plate edge pushes up against the other. When two plates collide under the sea, deep ocean trenches are made as one plate is forced under the other. Plates sliding past each other can cause earthquakes, as the rocks in the crust break and move. Most **volcanoes** and earthquakes happen along the boundaries of the Earth's plates.

# Earth

# Continents jigsaw

## WHAT YOU NEED

cardboard

poster board

paints and brush

scissors

black pen

pencil

paper fasteners

**1** Draw an outline of the world's continents onto a piece of poster board.

**2** Draw mountains, forests, and animals onto the continents, then paint the picture.

**3** Outline the continents with black pen, then cut them out to make the jigsaw puzzle pieces.

**4** Mount the cut-out map onto cardboard. Push paper fasteners through each jigsaw piece to make them easier to pick up and place.

You could make this fun jigsaw for a younger brother or sister

# Wrinkles and ridges

If you could see the Earth from far away in space, it would look like a giant, smooth ball. Yet we know that our planet is far from being smooth. Earth is covered with a rough, rocky surface called the crust. Tall mountain ranges stand above the land in high, sharp ridges and deep valleys cut grooves into the surface.

## Narrow chains

Mountains are usually joined in narrow chains of peaks, which may be thousands of miles long. The world's tallest mountain is Mount Everest. It is 29,029 feet (8,848 m) high and is part of the Himalaya mountain range in Asia. Although we cannot see them, there are also mountains under the oceans. A large mountain range runs down the middle of the Atlantic Ocean. It is called the Mid-Atlantic Ridge, and is longer than any mountain range on land.

## Rock piles

The peaks of a mountain range reach high into the **atmosphere**. It is too high for plants to grow and so cold that snow and ice cover the bare rock. The mountains themselves are made from large piles of twisted, folded rocks.

## A mountain grows

A mountain range forms when the separate, floating plates beneath the Earth's crust collide. When two plates push against each other, the rocks along each edge are forced together. The rock layers push up together and fold over and under each other.

# Earth

Build up a mountain range using real rock textures

## WHAT YOU NEED

cardboard strips

poster board

paper

pencil

sand

soil

small stones

glue

black paint and brush

scissors

crushed chalk

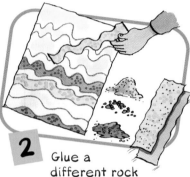

**1** Draw a sketch of mountain layers on paper.

**2** Glue a different rock material or cardboard strip in each layer.

**3** Paint lines for cracks running down from the surface.

**4** Cut along each layer, then glue them on poster board.

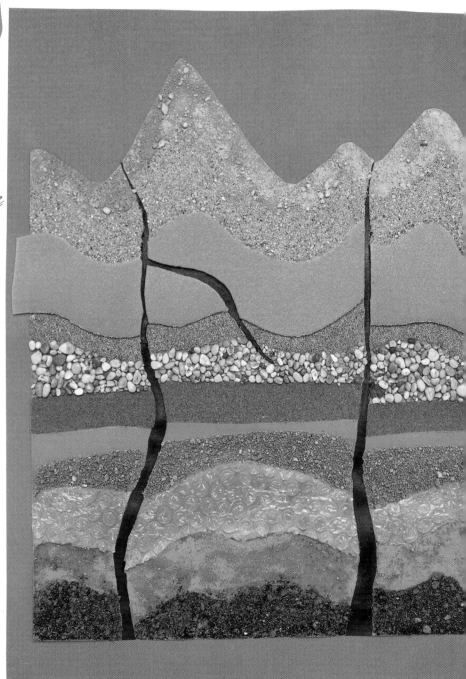

# Earthquake!

During an earthquake, the ground tears apart and buildings collapse.

Imagine if the ground under your feet suddenly started to tremble and a deep rumbling sound began roaring in your ears. You listen as buildings shake, windows shatter, cars turn over, and people are thrown to the ground. A huge crack splits the ground apart. You have witnessed an earthquake!

## Where in the world

The Earth's surface is made of slowly moving plates. Earthquakes occur in places where the plates meet, such as all around the coasts of the Pacific Ocean and in many parts of southern Europe. Central America and California are two places that also experience strong earthquakes.

## Waves and shakes

An earthquake happens when strong forces, called stresses, build up in the moving rocks deep underground. As the plates scrape past each other, the pressure grows, until suddenly the rocks bend and crack. A gigantic **shock wave** then spreads up and out, followed by more waves. The waves travel very fast – up to 15,534 miles (25,000 km) an hour. In the strongest earthquakes, you can see these waves moving the ground up and down.

## City destroyer

More than a million earthquakes happen around the world every year. Most of them are too weak to be felt, but the biggest earthquakes can do a lot of damage. Even the strongest earthquake lasts only about a minute or two, yet in that time, a whole city can be destroyed. If an earthquake happens under the ocean floor, it may cause a series of gigantic waves, called **tsunamis**. This wall of water can travel across the ocean surface and smash into the land.

# Earth

## WHAT YOU NEED

cardboard box

paint

glue

brush

tissue paper

scissors

glitter

sand

newspaper

pencil

poster board

# Sand box

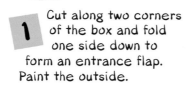

**1** Cut along two corners of the box and fold one side down to form an entrance flap. Paint the outside.

**2** Scrunch up newspaper to form a landscape and glue into the box along with tissue paper twists.

**3** Paint the inside different shades of yellow. When dry, glue sand and glitter on the base.

**4** On the poster board, draw and paint a variety of cacti.

**5** Paint these and decorate with glitter. Cut out and glue them onto your landscape.

You could glue colored sand over the base of your box for a decorative rainbow effect.

Add loose sand and colored pebbles. Shake the box from side to side to see the landscape shift

15

# Firecones

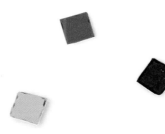

A volcano is a mountain that builds itself. Deep inside the Earth, it is so hot that there are pockets of melted rock, called **magma**, and gas. The gas forces the magma up through cracks in the Earth's crust. The magma is then called **lava**. It cools and becomes the black, gritty rock that builds the sides of the volcano.

## Lava and ash

A volcano erupts like a big fiery explosion. Sometimes a fountain of hot lava is shot high into the air, with clouds of dust, or ash, and gas. Rivers of lava can pour from cracks in the sides of the volcano. Sometimes, solid chunks of red-hot rock and cinders shoot out, or the eruption is so powerful that the whole volcano blows to pieces. If the lava is thin, it spreads out to make a wide, flat volcano, such as Mauna Loa in Hawaii. Thick lava builds into a cone-shaped volcano with steep sides, such as Mount Fuji in Japan.

## Asleep or awake?

There are several thousand volcanoes in the world, but most are **extinct**, which means that they do not erupt anymore. Others are **dormant**, or sleeping. Dormant volcanoes can erupt at any moment! An **active volcano** is one that is always erupting.

## Hot spots

Volcanoes are found both on dry land and under the sea. Many are found around the edge of the Pacific Ocean. These belong to a large group of volcanoes called the "Ring of Fire." Other volcanic "hot spots" include Hawaii and Iceland.

An erupting volcano sends fiery-hot lava shooting high into the air.

# Earth

Make your volcanic explosion look fierce and fiery!

## WHAT YOU NEED

paints and brush

small stones

sand

glue

container

pencil

colored construction paper

paper

spoon

toothbrush

**1** Stir sand, stones, and glue in the container to make a sticky mixture.

**2** Draw the outline of a volcano on paper. Brush on the lumpy glue mixture. Let it dry.

**3** Pour thinned paint around the top of the volcano. Tilt the paper backward and forward so the paint runs in different directions.

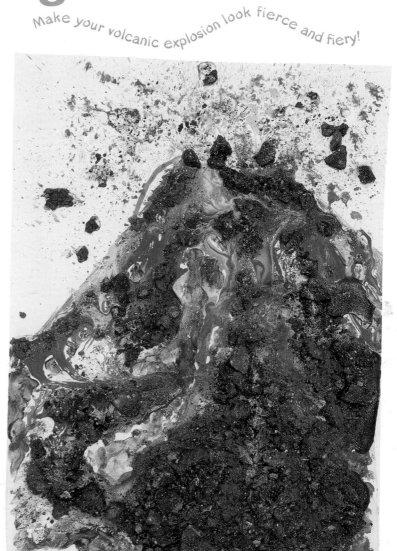

**4** Flick paint over your picture with the toothbrush and leave to dry. Mount on colored construction paper.

# Steam fountains

Inside the Earth it is so hot that the rocks are **molten**, like melted chocolate. Sometimes, molten rock and gas bursts through the surface as a volcano. Sometimes, a spray of hissing steam and hot water shoots up into a **geyser**. This heat also escapes as **fumaroles**, hot springs, and underwater smokers.

## Central heating

In some parts of the world, hot, molten rock lies close to the Earth's surface. These hot rocks heat up water trapped in the cooler layers of rock above them. This can be very useful. People in Iceland use volcanically heated water to make electricity. Volcanically heated water is also piped into towns.

## Springs and mud pools

Hot water sometimes bubbles up to the surface in springs. In New Zealand, people can swim in naturally warm, outdoor pools.

Mud pools form where spring water mixes with soil and sand. Bubbles of smelly **sulphur** gas erupt through the mud. They come from the volcanic magma rock underground. People often bathe in warm mud because they think it is good for their skin.

## Steam jets

In some places inside the Earth, water gets trapped a long way down. As it grows hotter, pressure builds up so that the boiling water starts to rise to the surface. Large spouts of steam and water shoot out of cracks in the Earth's crust and are sent high into the air. These steam jets are called geysers and they erupt regularly. Old Faithful is a geyser in Yellowstone Park in Wyoming. It spouts out a 184-foot (56 m) jet of water about every 30 minutes.

## Black smokers

Gases deep inside the Earth can also heat up and escape. Fumaroles are found near volcanoes, in places where gases come out of the Earth. Under the oceans, fumaroles called black smokers belch out hot water and gases into the sea.

# Earth

# Geysers and fumaroles

paints and brush

small stones

cotton balls

small clear plastic bags

white paint

toothbrush

cardboard

scissors

blue tissue paper

glue

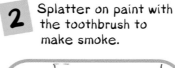

**2** Splatter on paint with the toothbrush to make smoke.

**1** Paint a volcanic landscape on cardboard. Fold base.

**3** Paint steamy jets with dabs of white and blue paint using a dry brush.

**4** Glue cotton balls to cardboard to make a fumarole. Fold at the bottom so it stands up and glue in place.

**5** Glue blue tissue paper strips onto a small plastic bag to make a geyser. Scrunch it up and glue onto the base

Create a steamy stand-up scene of gushing geysers and strange, smoking fumaroles

Pile small stones around the base of your geysers and fumaroles to make them stand up.

19

# Striped layers

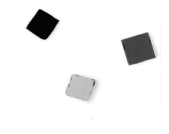

W hen the Earth first formed, it was a boiling hot, swirling ball of melted rock and metal dust. As it cooled, the heaviest materials, the nickel and iron, sank to the middle to make the center, called the core. Next, a deep layer of soft rock, called the mantle, settled around the core. Finally, Earth's rock-hard, outer covering formed. This is called the crust.

## Melted minerals

The first rocks on Earth all formed from liquid. They rose to the surface from the mantle and cooled. These cooled rocks are called **igneous rocks**. They are made from minerals, the small pieces in a rock that are different shapes and colors. Granite is a kind of igneous rock. Basalt is the igneous rock that flows from volcanoes as liquid lava.

## Wear and tear

As soon as the first rain fell on Earth, the surface rocks began to wear away. The igneous rocks broke down into pebbles, sand, **silt**, and mud. Water carried the pieces away to form beaches, river deltas, and mudflats. The pieces settled in layers and very slowly formed new rock, called **sedimentary rock**.

## Changing shape

The Earth is always wearing away old rocks and forming new ones. Igneous and sedimentary rocks can change into **metamorphic rock**. This happens when they heat up, or are covered by layers of other rocks. Heat and weight make rocks change. Slate and marble are examples of metamorphic rock.

Sandstone formations in Utah, USA.

# Earth

## Pebble pictures

### WHAT YOU NEED

smooth stones

pencil

paints and brush

PVA
glue

**2** Draw a simple scene or animal outline and paint it on the stones.

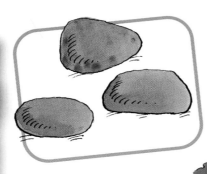

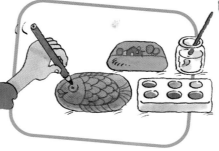

**1** Collect some different shaped smooth stones.

**3** When dry, varnish with PVA glue mixed with a little water.

*These colorful painted pebbles make great presents for friends!*

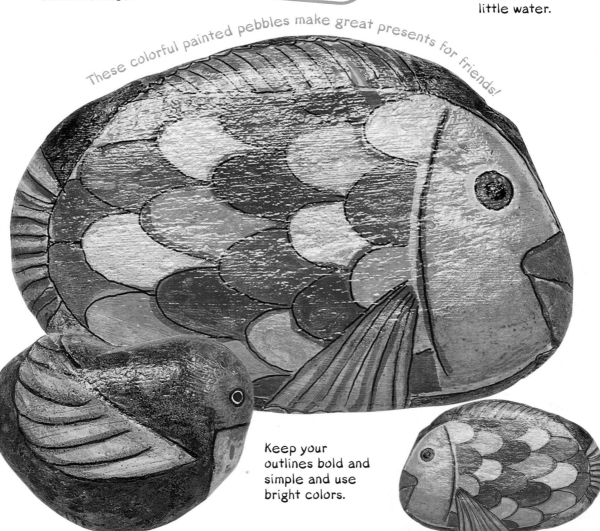

Keep your outlines bold and simple and use bright colors.

21

# Fossil features

Fossils are rocks that contain the shape, or parts, of animals and plants that lived long ago. They can also be the footprints an animal left behind. We usually think of dinosaur bones, which are millions of years old, as the best examples of fossils. In fact, fossils of animals that lived on the land are actually quite rare. Most plants and animals that became fossilized lived in or near water.

## Watery graves

An animal or plant can only become a fossil if it has some hard body parts. For example, shellfish, crabs, and lobsters have hard shells; fish, turtles, and crocodiles have bony skeletons, teeth, and scales. Water plants have tough stems. It is also important to be in or near water because sand and mud collect at the bottom of lakes, rivers, seas, and oceans. When a dead plant or animal sinks to the bottom, it is buried and the mud protects it.

## Surprise fossils

Fossils of land-living animals are more rare. If a dinosaur died near a river, or got stuck in quicksand on a beach, it had a better chance of becoming a fossil. Soft-bodied animals, such as jellyfish or worms, are very rare fossils. Some surprising things are tough enough to fossilize – these include leaves, insect wings, and feathers. Animal burrows and trails can also become fossils.

## Clues to the past

Fossils tell us about plants and animals that once lived on Earth. By studying them, scientists have been able to build a picture of life in **prehistoric times**, even before the dinosaurs. The oldest fossils ever found are microscopic traces of **bacteria** cells in rock. Scientists believe these bacteria lived about three and a half billion years ago!

# Earth

# Fossil find

## WHAT YOU NEED

clay

paints

wooden stick or end of a paint brush

**2** Use the wooden stick to give the fossils different textures and patterns.

**1** Roll clay and shape into swirled, shell-like fossil shapes, as shown.

**3** Leave clay to dry and then paint your fossils.

Display your fossils in a sandy seabed. Add some shiny stones as decorations

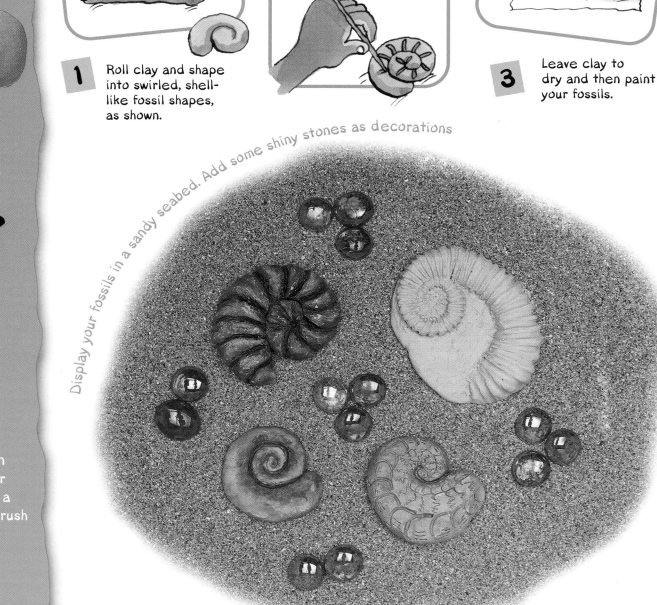

23

# Oil, coal, and gas

**O**ur planet provides many of the materials that we use in daily life. Since their discovery, **fossil fuels** buried deep underground have been the most useful source of power. Fossil fuels come from the remains of dead plants and animals that lived millions of years ago. Oil, coal, and gas are the main fossil fuels. They supply energy to make electricity and fuel to drive our cars.

## Coal from plants

Millions of years ago, many parts of the world were covered by swamps and forests. When dead plants and trees fell to the ground, they sank into the mud. Other trees and plants fell on top, forming a thick layer of dead plants. In time, these plants rotted to form lumpy, brown peat. Later, the peat was buried under tons of water, mud, and sand. All this weight eventually turned the peat into coal.

## Oil and gas

Oil and gas were also made from dead **organisms**. Millions of years ago, when tiny plants and animals living in the seas died, they drifted down to the seabed. The weight of sand and mud settling over the layers slowly squeezed them together and changed them into oil and gas. Today, people drill down through layers of rock to find the pools of oil and supplies of gas.

## Limited supplies

The Earth has only a limited supply of fossil fuels. Once they are used up, they cannot be replaced. Scientists are trying to find alternative fuels, so that fossil fuels can be conserved.

# Earth

# Textured oil painting

## WHAT YOU NEED

oil paints

fork

spatula or palette knife

paper

cardboard or poster board

glue

paintbrush

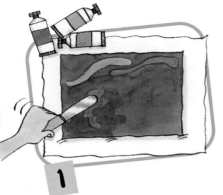

**1** Choose dark colors for the background of your painting. Use a spatula or palette knife to spread the paint evenly.

**2** Add dabs and swirls of bright paint onto your paper. With a fork, the end of a brush, or other tool, draw patterns and shapes in the paint.

**3** When your picture is dry, mount it on cardboard or poster board.

See and feel the textures in the colorful patterns of your painting

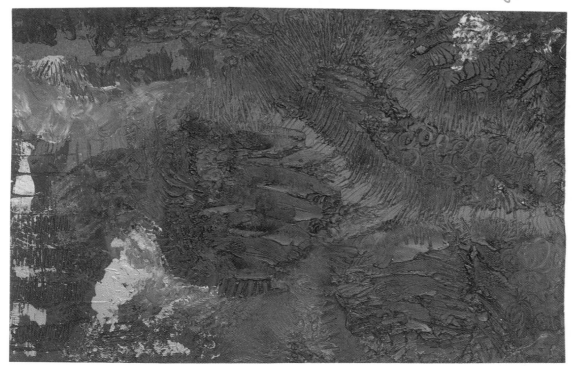

# Shifting sands

Deserts are dry, barren places where hardly any rain falls. They can be covered by sand, dried mud, or gravel and rocks. Some, such as the Sahara in Africa, are scorching hot all the time.

Others, such as the Gobi Desert in Asia, are freezing in winter. In sandy deserts, strong winds pile the sand into high ridges, called dunes. As the wind blows, the sand dunes are always changing shape.

## Stars and crescents

A barchan sand dune is crescent-shaped and a seif is a curving wave. Some dunes make a star shape, and others make long, straight lines. Because the dunes are always changing shape, a desert has no landmarks, so travelers can easily lose their way. Sand dunes in the Arabian desert can be 787 feet (240 m) high. The middle of the Kalahari desert in Southern Africa looks like a sandy sea of red sand dunes.

## Rocky deserts

Rocky deserts, such as those in North America, are places where the wind has carved strange-shaped rocks. In Death Valley, California, temperatures can reach more than 133°F (56°C). The Atacama Desert in Chile is the world's driest desert. It sometimes does not rain there for years.

## Survivors

Desert plants and animals are specially designed for life in such a hostile place. Most animals only come out in the cool evening. They get moisture from the morning dew, from eating other animals, and from plants that store water in their leaves and stems.

The ridge of a dune in Namib Naukluft Park, Namibia.

# Earth

*Create a colorful desert scene with sandy dune shapes*

## WHAT YOU NEED

sand

crushed chalk

sandpaper

paper

glue

scissors

paints and brush

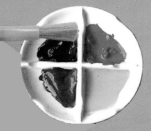

poster board or cardboard

pencil

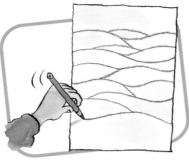

**1** Draw an outline of desert dunes onto your paper.

**2** Cut dune shapes from sandpaper. Glue sandpaper, chalk, and sand onto sections of the paper.

**3** Leave some surfaces plain. Paint others in different desert colors. Leave to dry.

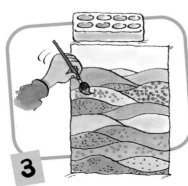

Make your dunes sparkle in the dry desert heat by sprinkling some layers with red or gold glitter.

**4** Cut out the picture and mount on poster board.

27

# Rock sculptures

The combined forces of water, wind, and ice wear away at the Earth's surface over time. In the United States, the Colorado River has been cutting through Arizona's landscape for about six million years. It has dug a deep, steep-sided valley called the Grand Canyon. The amazing sculpted rocks were shaped by the water wearing them away.

## On the attack

Year by year, over millions of years, the weather attacks the land. It wears down mountains into hills, hills into plains, and cuts channels through the land. This process is called **erosion**. Weather can even crack rocks. High on a mountain, water seeps into tiny cracks in the rock. At night, the water can freeze. Because ice takes up more space than water, it forces the crack open. Finally, a piece of rock splits off and rolls away.

## Dry deserts

In some deserts, temperatures can quickly change from scorching hot in the day to freezing cold at night. After a time, these changes in temperature loosen the rock layers until a layer peels away. In sandy deserts, when the wind blows strongly, the sand is blasted against hillsides. Over millions of years, this can create fantastic rock sculptures, holes, and arches.

## Cliffs and caves

Water pounding away at the land can also carve shapes into cliffs. A hollow at the foot of the cliff slowly gets bigger and deeper until, finally, a deep cave is formed.

The Grand Canyon.

## Earth

**WHAT YOU NEED**

clay

paints and brush

wooden stick or paintbrush handle

sequins

PVA glue

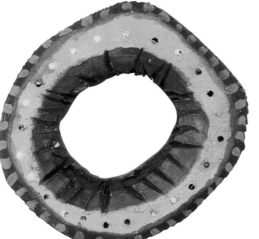

**1** Roll the clay into round shapes. Make holes in the middle by pushing the clay with your thumb.

Display your pebble carvings on a windowsill or place them around indoor plants, such as cacti.

*Make and decorate these weird and wonderful weathered shapes*

**2** Add ridges, hollows, cracks, and small holes with a thin wooden stick. Add sequins for decoration.

**3** When dry, paint and decorate your pebble carvings. Varnish them with a mixture of PVA glue and water.

# Stone icicles

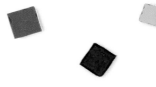

Have you ever been inside a cave and saw what looked like giant stone icicles? Some hang down from the roof of the cave. Others stick up from the floor. These strange-looking cones are usually found inside limestone caves.

## Growing down

The cones that hang down are called **stalactites**. They are made by water trickling through the roof of the cavern. The water is full of dissolved lime which forms a mineral called calcite. The calcite sticks onto the ceiling and a cone begins to grow.

## Growing up

On the cave floor, the same thing happens, but the other way around. As the water from the roof drips onto the floor, little piles of calcite build up. Cones that stick up from the floor are called **stalagmites**.

## Meeting point

Often water drips off the end of a stalactite onto the top of a stalagmite underneath. Very slowly, the two grow toward each other until they finally join. It is easy to get stalactites and stalagmites mixed up! You can remember which is which if you think of "c" for ceiling (stalactite) and "g" for ground (stalagmite).

# Earth

## WHAT YOU NEED

two small cardboard boxes

brush

silver paint

black paint

newspaper

glue

scissors

tin foil

clear tape

glitter

needle and thread

**1** Cut a semi-circle from each box and stick the boxes together to form a round hole at the front.

**2** Glue crumpled newspaper to the outside of the box and paint it silver and black.

**3** Twist tin foil into long cones for stalactites and stalagmites. Cover with glue and sprinkle on glitter.

**4** Attach thread to some of the cones. Tape these to the top of the cave for stalactites. Stick the rest to the cave floor for stalagmites.

Look at the stalagmites and stalactites shining in the dark!

Decorate the scene with small pebbles.

# Iron and bronze

Copper was probably the first metal that people learned to shape, but it was too soft to make any strong or sharp tools or weapons. Metalworkers later found that by mixing copper with tin, they could make a much harder metal called bronze. Later, iron was discovered. Iron was tough, strong, and easy to shape into sharp edges and points.

## The Bronze Age

A mixture of different metals is called an **alloy**. The alloy bronze was first made about 5,000 years ago. Its discovery marked the beginning of a time in history called the **Bronze Age**. At first, bronze was only known in a few countries, but it soon became the main material for making tools and weapons. Metalworkers could also **cast** or shape it into delicate jewelry and ceremonial objects. Shining, polished bronze was a sign of wealth and power.

## Precious ore

Metals come from minerals in rocks called ores. During the Bronze Age, the sites where copper and tin ores could be found became very important. They were owned by the most powerful lords and kings. These precious ores were traded by different nations.

## The Iron Age

About 3,500 years ago, iron began to replace bronze. This tough metal made stronger tools and weapons. Iron ores were also more common than tin and copper. Iron mining was extremely hard work. The ore had to be dug out of the ground using hand tools. Then it was smelted. This means the rocks were crushed and heated in furnaces until the iron melted and flowed out as a thick liquid. When the iron cooled, it changed into a hard, dull-looking black metal. The Iron Age has never really ended. Iron is still a very important metal in today's world. We make the alloy steel from iron. We use steel to make hundreds of objects, from safety pins to skyscrapers, scissors to engine parts, and bridges to buildings.

An iron ore mine at Pilbara, Australia.

# Earth

## WHAT YOU NEED

cardboard box with lid

silver paint

gold and silver metallic paper

brush

wooden toggle

scissors

corrugated cardboard

glue

paper fasteners

metal buttons

wire

# Strongbox

**1** Glue corrugated cardboard on two sides of the box and metallic paper on the top. Paint silver.

**2** Glue strips of gold paper along all the edges.

**3** Cut a door out of the top and push paper fasteners into the box along the gold paper edges.

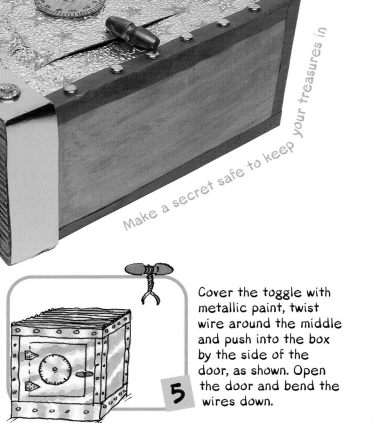

Glue a wider strip of metallic paper around one edge and glue on some metal buttons.

*Make a secret safe to keep your treasures in*

**4** Make a dial and hinges from cardboard. Glue the hinges at one side of the door and attach the dial with a paper fastener.

**5** Cover the toggle with metallic paint, twist wire around the middle and push into the box by the side of the door, as shown. Open the door and bend the wires down.

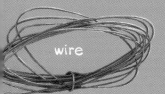

# Gemstones

Gemstones, or jewels, are beautiful natural minerals. They are found in rocks in the Earth's crust. Since ancient times, people have collected them to make jewelry or ornaments. Sapphires, rubies, emeralds, and diamonds are the most expensive gemstones.

## Earth's treasures

Some gemstones are very difficult to find. They form up to 124 miles (200 km) underground, where layers of rock are squeezed very tightly together and the temperature is very high. Some stones may be 3,000 million years old. Diamonds are the most valuable of all the gemstones. In the past, many of the largest and most famous diamonds were dug from the Kimberley mine in South Africa. The miners who found them risked their lives to bring them to the surface. Not all diamonds are good enough to be used for jewelry. They must be exactly the right color, shape, and weight.

## Hard and tough

Beautiful gemstones that are more easily found are called semi-precious stones. They include topaz, amethyst, opal, and spinel. The best gems are beautiful, rare, and hard. They need to be tough if they are to be used in rings, necklaces, and brooches. Diamond is the hardest substance of all – it can even cut rocks. Gems also have to be a good color, with no faults, or flaws, in them.

## Sparkling jewels

Have you ever watched the jewel in a ring or necklace sparkle as it catches the light? Before they are cut and polished, even the most precious gemstones look dull! Jewelers use diamond-tipped saws to cut stones into shapes that will make them sparkle. They use diamond dust to polish the stones into brilliant shining gems.

# Earth

### WHAT YOU NEED

clay

paints

paint brush

beads

**1**

Roll long lengths from the clay. Coil one around to make the base and pile the rest on top of each other to make the sides.

**2**

Use your fingers to push the clay together to form a smooth surface.

**3**

Decorate your bowl by pushing beads into the sides. Leave to dry.

**4**

Paint the bowl inside and out.

Jewels inside and out – use this precious bowl to keep your jewelry in!

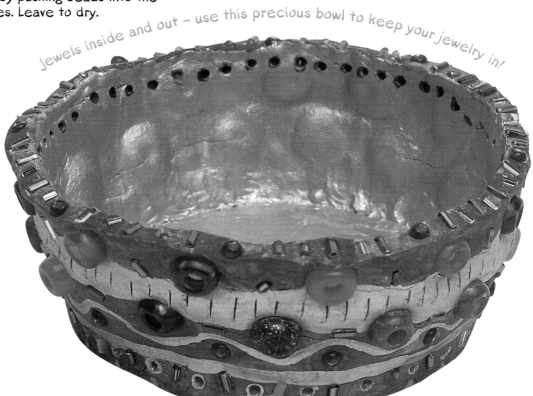

# Marvelous metals

What do an airplane and a soft-drink can have in common? Both are made from a light, strong metal known as aluminum. Aluminum is one of many different metals that exist in the rocks of the Earth's crust. We have found many uses for these metals. Some are even melted down and combined.

## Amazing ores

Pure metal is very rare. Gold, silver, copper, and mercury are about the only examples of pure metals. Gold is thought to be the earliest metal discovered. All other metals are found as minerals – the natural non-living material that makes up rocks. These valuable minerals are called ores. To separate the metals, the ores have to be mined and heated to very high temperatures. This is called **smelting.**

Extremely high temperatures cause sparks to fly at this copper smelting plant in Chile.

## Super alloys

Most metals we use today are alloys, which are metals mixed together when they are molten, or melted. Steel is an alloy of iron and other metals. Steel can be mixed with non-metals, such as nickel, chromium, or carbon, to make new materials. Gold alloyed with silver and platinum is harder and stronger than gold by itself. Many metals are used for specific purposes because of their attributes. Tin does not rust, so it is used to make cans for food. Copper conducts electricity, so it is used to make wire.

# Earth

## WHAT YOU NEED

pencil

glue

wire

cardboard

silver foil

metallic paint

brush

bolts, chains, and screws

# Metal collage

Use metal objects and paper to create a shiny wall picture!

**1** Use your pencil and paints to divide a piece of cardboard into squares and rectangles. Glue foil on some of these shapes.

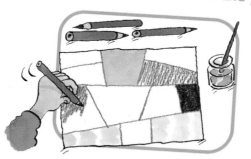

**2** Glue on metal screws, nuts, and bolts.

**3** Thread pieces of wire around the metal objects to decorate your picture and give it a "mechanical" look!

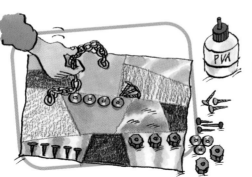

# Silver and gold

Of all the metals, gold and silver are the most precious. They were among the first metals discovered and used by humans. The bright yellow metal of gold and the soft white metal of silver were prized for their beauty and rarity. They were used to make beautiful jewelry, ornaments, and coins. Gold was especially prized because, unlike silver, it does not lose its shine over time.

## Nuggets and wires

Gold and silver come from the earth. They are mined from rocks and separated out so that they can either be used in their pure forms or mixed with other metals. In the past, gold and silver were found as natural crystals and grains. Lumps, or nuggets, of gold were found in the beds of streams and rivers, where they had been washed out of the earth by the water. Gold-diggers would use shallow dishes to "pan", or sieve them from the water. Silver is found as crystals that look like threads of wire set in the rock. It used to be dug from mines and quarries. Today, gold and silver-bearing rock is crushed and the metals are taken out, or **extracted**, by chemical methods. It takes 6,614 pounds (3 tons) of rock to produce one ounce (32 g) of gold!

## Incredible metals

Gold and silver are known as "soft" metals. They are soft because 1.1 ounces (32 g) of gold can be pulled into a wire 25 miles (40 km) long. Gold that has been rolled flat, beaten, and cut, over and over again, is known as gold leaf. One thousand leaves of gold will be as thick as this page. Gold leaf has been used to decorate carvings, masks, picture frames, and even buildings. Today, gold and silver are often mixed with other metals to make them harder. A mix of metals alloyed with silver is used to make knives and other cutlery.

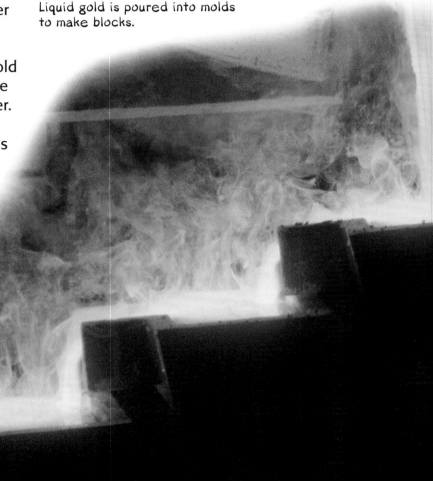

Liquid gold is poured into molds to make blocks.

# Earth

# Golden mask

## WHAT YOU NEED

poster board

scissors

pencil

gold paint
and brush

string

glue

**1** Draw the outline and facial features of your mask on the poster board.

**2** Glue string over the facial features, as shown.

**3** Paint your mask gold.

**4** Cut out the mask.

Make a collection of masks for your bedroom wall. Use gold or silver paint

You can also add beautiful beads to decorate your mask and make it shine!

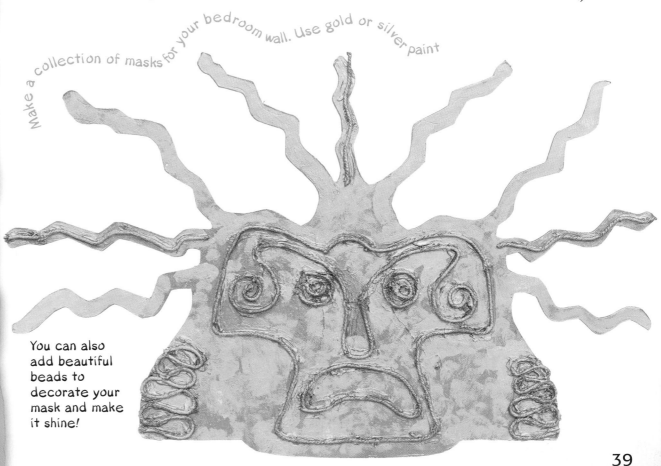

39

# Mottled marble

Next time you visit a museum, a gallery, or even the shopping mall, look out for cool, beautiful marble. Marble is a rock we use for building and decorating the inside of big or important places, such as museums. Marble comes in many colors, and has a mottled pattern of ripples and streaks that is easy to recognize.

## Rock from the sea

Marble was once a type of rock called limestone. Over time, it was changed by pressure into marble. Limestone formed millions of years ago under the seas and oceans, from layer upon layer of dead sea animals. Eventually, the limestone rock sank deep into the Earth, where it changed into new kinds of rock. Then, as new mountain ranges were pushed up onto the Earth's surface, the new rocks came up too and formed part of the land.

## Stone quarries

The marble and other rocks we use for building come from stone quarries.

The rock is dug, or cut out of the ground using special tools and equipment. Because marble is easy to cut and shape, it is known as a soft rock. At first, raw marble can look very ordinary. It must be cut and polished to bring out the ripples and streaks.

## Cool beauty

Many of the world's marble quarries are in Europe, especially in Italy. Long ago, the ancient Romans chose marble to build with because it looked beautiful and also because the cold stone kept their homes cool in summer. Marble is "soft" and, therefore, is a good rock to carve. The ancient Greeks carved statues from marble. Today, many sculptors still prefer to use only the finest, unmarked, white marble for carving.

# Earth

## WHAT YOU NEED

oil paints

turpentine

glue

paper

poster board

tub and water

brush

crayons

plastic containers

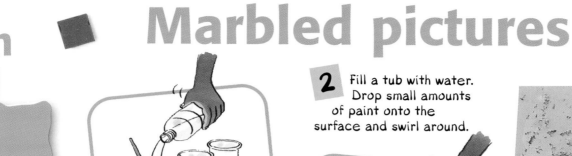

**1** Mix various colored paints in containers, each with a small amount of turpentine. Always ask an adult to help you when you use turpentine.

**2** Fill a tub with water. Drop small amounts of paint onto the surface and swirl around.

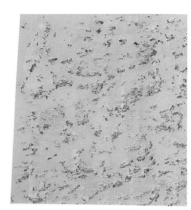

*Achieve dramatic marble effects with paint and water*

**3** Place paper on top of the water to pick up the pattern floating on top.

**4** When dry, mount on poster board. Repeat using different colored paints.

**5** You can also make rubbings from rocks using wax crayons to create the same effect.

# Clay soldiers

Imagine an army of more than 7,000 warriors with their chariots and horses, standing row after row, silent and still. This is China's Terracotta Army: thousands of clay statues which had been buried for over 2,000 years. Ancient Chinese Emperor Qin had them made to escort him into the **afterlife**. The statues were originally painted with natural mineral and plant colors, but after their long burial in red, clay soil, the statues became the color of terracotta.

## Clay colors

Earth-colored clay comes from the ground beneath our feet. It is a mixture of extremely small bits of soil, alumina and silica minerals, and water. Other materials in the clay may give it a variety of colors. For example, iron oxide colors it red. Clay is a natural building material. We can shape it into cups, bowls, bricks, tiles, ornaments, and figures, which can be painted and decorated with patterns.

## Crushed earth

Long ago, cave artists painted with orange, yellow, brown, and black paints made from ground-up rocks and soil. Later, people used many natural materials for making colors. These included brightly colored minerals, and **dyes** from plants and animals. The ancient Egyptians took colorful natural minerals, such as green malachite and red cinnabar, and crushed them to make colors for make-up.

Rows of clay soldiers form the Terracotta Army.

# Earth

newspaper

paste

paint and brush

bowls

oil

# Terracotta pots

Use papier mâché to make a stunning collection of big and small pots

**1** Select a variety of bowls and coat the outside of them with oil.

**2** Tear strips of newspaper. Paste several layers onto the outside of the pots.

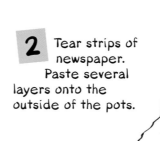

**3** When dry, remove the newspaper mold from the bowl. Paint the paper pots inside and out in a terracotta color: mix red and yellow paints together to make the correct color.

# Poles apart

The Earth spins on its axis, an imaginary line running from the North to the South Pole. The axis is tilted at an angle. This means that as Earth travels around, or **orbits**, the Sun, the amount of sunlight reaching its surface changes through the year. This gives many parts of the world their different seasons. In the polar regions, when the Earth's axis is tilted away from the Sun, there is no sunlight. When the axis is tilted toward the Sun, there is constant sunlight. The Poles get six months of day, then six months of night each year.

## Sea of ice

The north polar region is in the Arctic Circle, which lies thousands of miles north of the equator. This region is mostly made up of a sheet of ice lying on top of the Arctic Ocean, with some land around its edge. As the seasons change, the size of this ice island shrinks and grows. In the summer months, some of the ice melts or breaks off to form **icebergs.** In winter, the ice builds up again.

## Ice continent

The south polar region lies within the Antarctic Circle, the area that is farthest south from the Equator. The continent of Antarctica takes up most of this region. Antarctica is the coldest land mass on Earth. The only people living there are the scientists who work at the many research bases.

Only a small part of an iceberg is visible above the water, making them very dangerous for ocean ships.

# Earth

## Icy polar scene

### WHAT YOU NEED

filler paste

cardboard

scraps of fabric

gluestick

bowl

newspaper

scissors

poster board

pencil crayons

paints and brush

**1** Scrunch up newspaper into large balls and glue them onto the cardboard.

**2** Mix the filler paste in an old bowl or bucket, following the instructions on the package.

**3** Cut the fabric into postcard-size pieces. Dip these one by one into the plaster mixture and lay them over the newspaper mounds.

**4** Use the remaining plaster to cover the cardboard and fill in any gaps.

**5** On poster board, draw outlines of penguins, seals, and other polar animals. (Remember what poles they are from.) Color them and cut them out. Glue them around your polar scene.

Which polar animals will live in your icy landscape?

45

# Glossary

**active volcano** A volcano that still erupts.

**afterlife** The life some people believe follows death.

**alloy** A metallic material, such as steel, consisting of a mixture metals.

**atmosphere** A layer of gas that surrounds the outside of a planet or star.

**axis** The imaginary line through a spinning object such as a planet, around which the object rotates, or turns.

**bacteria** Tiny one-celled organisms. Some bacteria cause diseases and others help digest food.

**Bronze Age** A period of human civilization where people made things, such as weapons, from iron.

**cast** To shape a liquid metal by pouring it into a mold.

**continent** A huge area of land. Earth has seven continents: Africa, Antarctica, Asia, Australia, Europe, North and South America.

**crust** The outer, rocky layer of Earth on which the oceans and land lie.

**dormant volcano** An inactive volcano that is neither erupting, nor extinct.

**dyes** Substances that are used to stain or color fabrics and other materials.

**Equator** An imaginary line that circles Earth halfway between its North and South Poles.

**erosion** The wearing away of rocks and other materials on the Earth's surface by wind, water, or ice.

**extinct volcano** A volcano that will never erupt again.

**extract** To remove something from an object.

**fossil fuels** Any naturally occurring carbon or hydrocarbon fuel, such as coal or petroleum, that is formed from the fossilized remains of plants and animals.

**fumaroles** Vents in, or near, a volcano out of which comes hot gas.

**geyser** A natural hot spring. Hot water and steam shoot out of a hole in the Earth's crust at regular intervals.

**iceberg** A large piece of ice floating in the sea that has broken off a glacier or an ice sheet.

**igneous rock** A rock formed when hot liquid magma or lava cools and hardens, above or below the ground.

**lava** The name given to magma when it reaches the surface of the Earth.

**lines of latitude** Imaginary lines that run horizontally around the Earth. The Equator is at 0° and the lines of latitude measure the distance from the Equator in a north and south direction. The poles are at 90°.

**lines of longitude** Imaginary lines that run at right angles (90°) to the Equator and meet at the North and South Poles. These lines measure distance in degrees east or west around the Earth.

**magma** Hot, molten, or liquid, rock in the Earth's mantle and crust.

**mantle** The layer of soft rock that lies beneath the Earth's crust and surrounds the Earth's core.

**metamorphic rock** The rock formed when igneous or sedimentary rocks are changed by heat or pressure.

**molten** Liquefied, or melted.

**North Pole** The northernmost point on the Earth's axis.

**orbit** The curved path of travel of an object around a larger object in space.

**organisms** Living things, such as plants and animals.

**Pangaea** The name given to the ancient formation of Earth's continents.

**plate** A large rigid section of the Earth's surface, made up of the crust and upper section of the mantle. The Earth's surface is made up of about twelve different plates that are slowly moving.

**prehistoric times** The time before people began recording events in writing.

**sedimentary rock** A rock formed from the particles of other rocks, or from the remains of animals and plants.

**shock wave** The tremors that follow an earthquake.

**silt** Particles of mud or clay that collect together, especially at the mouth of a river or in a lake.

**smelting** Extracting, or removing, the metals from rock by heating the rocks.

**South Pole** The southernmost point on the Earth's axis.

**stalactites** Columns of calcite that hang down from the roof of a limestone cave.

**stalagmites** Columns of calcite that grow up from the floor of a limestone cave.

**sulphur** A gas with a strong, rotten-egg smell.

**symbols** A mark or picture used to represent something else.

**tsunamis** Gigantic waves that sweep across the ocean following an underwater earthquake.

**volcano** An opening in the Earth's crust through which lava and hot gases flow.

# Index

active volcano 16, 46
alloys 32, 36, 38, 46
aluminum 36, 42
Antarctic Circle 4, 44
Arctic Circle 4, 44
atmosphere 12, 46
axis 8, 44, 46

basalt 20
bronze 32

calcite 30
cast 32, 46
caves 28, 30-31, 42
clay 42
cliffs 28
coal 24
continents 10, 11, 44, 46
copper 32, 36
core 6, 20, 32

crust 6, 10, 12, 16, 20, 34, 36

deserts 26-28
diamonds 34
dinosaurs 22
dormant volcano 16, 46
dunes 26
dyes 42, 46

earthquakes 10, 14-15
Egyptians 42
Equator 4, 8, 46
erosion 28, 46
extinct volcano 16, 46
extracting metals 38

fossil fuels 24, 46
fossils 10, 22-23
fumaroles 18, 19, 46

gas (fossil fuel) 24
gases 16, 18
gemstones 34
geysers 18, 19, 46
gold 36, 38
Grand Canyon 28

hot springs 18

ice damage 28
icebergs 44, 46
igneous rocks 20, 46
iron 20, 32, 36

lava 16, 20
limestone 30, 40
lines of latitude 4, 46
lines of longitude 4, 46

magma 16, 18, 46
mantle 6, 10, 20, 46
maps 4
marble 40
metals 6, 36-37, 38
metamorphic rock 20, 46
minerals 20, 30, 34, 36, 42
mines 32, 34, 38

molten rock 18
Moon 8, 9
mountains 10, 12-13, 16, 28, 40
mud pools 18

nickel 20, 36
North Pole 4, 44, 46

oceans 10, 12, 14
oil 24
Old Faithful 18
orbit 44, 46
ores 32, 36

Pangaea 10, 46
plates 10, 12, 14, 46

quarries 38, 40

rock sculptures 28

sand box 15
sand dunes 26-27
sandstone 20
seasons 8, 44
sedimentary rock 20, 46
shock waves 14, 46
silver 36, 38

smelting 36, 46
South Pole 4, 44, 46
stalactites 30-31, 46
stalagmite 30-31, 46
steel 32, 36
sulphur 18, 46
Sun 8, 9, 44

Terracotta Army 42
textured oil painting 25
tin 32, 36
tsunamis 14, 46

volcanoes 10, 16-17, 18, 46

47

# Materials guide

A list of materials, how to use them, and suitable alternatives

WHAT YOU NEED

gold foil

silver foil

filler paste

PVA glue

flour

salt

cellophane or acetate

The crafts in this book require the use of materials and products that are easily purchased in craft stores. If you cannot locate some materials, you can substitute other materials with those we have listed here, or use your imagination to make the craft with what you have on hand.

**Gold foil:** can be found in craft stores. It is very delicate and sometimes tears.

**Silver foil:** can be found in craft stores. It is very delicate, soft and sometimes tears. For some crafts, tin or aluminum foil can be substituted. Aluminum foil is a less delicate material and makes a harder finished craft.

**PVA glue:** commonly called polyvinyl acetate. It is a modeling glue that creates a type of varnish when mixed with water. It is also used as a strong glue. In some crafts, other strong glues can be substituted, and used as an adhesive, but not as a varnish.

**Filler paste:** sometimes called plaster of Paris. It is a paste that hardens when it dries. It can be purchased at craft and hardware stores.

**Paste:** a paste of 1/2 cup flour, one tablespoon of salt and one cup of warm water can be made to paste strips of newspaper as in a papier mâché craft. Alternatively, wallpaper paste can be purchased and mixed as per directions on the package.

**Cellophane:** a clear or colored plastic material. Acetate can also be used in crafts that call for this material. Acetate is a clear, or colored, thin plastic that can be found in craft stores.

1 2 3 4 5 6 7 8 9 0   Printed in the USA   0 9 8 7 6 5 4 3 2